Workbook for Bill Perkins'
Die With Zero

Printed Exercises for Optimizing, Planning and Actioning the Lessons

 BIG ACTION BOOKS

BigActionBooks.com

Contents

Introduction

Ready to action "Die With Zero", to get the most out of life? Let's get to work.

WHY THIS WORKBOOK?

You've read Bill Perkins' excellent book about how to plan out your finances and experiences to get the most out of life - without sacrificing the present. Now it's time to actually practice it - write, journal, and put the lessons in motion.

This workbook was created as a **companion** to Bill Perkins' *"Die With Zero"*. While reading the book, we found ourselves wishing for a place where we could write, process and practice the book's exercises and recommendations in a constructive, concise way. The exercises are excellent - but there isn't much space to actually write in the book itself. Instead, we found ourselves cobbling them together in various places - notebooks, journals, pieces of paper - all of which would eventually get lost, or at the very least, not be helpful in putting the lessons into practice. That's how this workbook was born.

HOW TO USE THIS WORKBOOK

This workbook is like a faithful friend to *Die with Zero*. In it, you'll find exactly what's advertised: the exercises from the book, summarized and formatted, with space to answer.

- All exercises from Die With Zero -- from the back of each chapter under "Recommendations" -- extracted into one single place
- Space to write under each exercise
- Lists, ruled lines and space for you to answer, journal and reflect
- Clearly organized and well-formatted so it's easy to follow

We've extracted the main premise of the exercise, and added space to respond and practice the lessons. This may come in the format of a table to fill in, space to free-write, or other exercise methods to provide space for reflection. The book's chapters are also referenced throughout, so you can easily find a specific section for further context.

If you're ready to reevaluate your finances and your experience, to create a fulfilling life worth living - and die with zero so you've lived to the fullest - this workbook, as well as your own dedication, will help you do just that.

Enjoy, and thank you.
Let's dive in!

---

* Please note: This is an unofficial workbook companion for Die With Zero to help motivated do-ers process the lessons from this fantastic book. It is not created by or associated with Bill Perkins in any official way.

Chapter 1: Optimize Your Life

Rule No.1: Maximize your positive life experiences.

Which Experiences Would Enrich Your Life?

Begin actively thinking about the experiences in your life that you'd like to have, and how many times you'd like to have them. They could be big or small; expensive or free; to help others such as charities, or solely for you such as a flashy new sports car. Think about what you'd *really* like to get out of this life and what would be memorable for you.

These could be general, or might relate to a specific category of experience like health, friends, family or travel. Below, we've listed several important categories that might help you craft your ideal experience list. You can also ignore the categories (if you prefer) and make your own list from scratch.

Potential experience categories:

- Friends & Family
- Experiences & adventure
- Health & fitness
- Work

- Hobbies & personal expression
- Self-improvement
- Giving
- Spirituality

Experiences I'd like to have - fill out your own, below:

Category (optional)	Experience	No. of times
Example: Health & Fitness	Example: Run a marathon	Example: 2

(Continued...)

Category (optional)	Experience	No. of times

Notes/insights from the above:

_____

_____

_____

_____

_____

_____

_____

_____

Chapter 2: Invest in experiences
Rule No. 2: Start investing in experiences early.

Early... is right now

Remember - "early" is the same as right now. Of the experiences you noted down in the exercise above, consider which ones would be best to invest in today, this month, or this year. If you encounter some resistance to having them right now, also consider the opposite: what is the risk of <u>not</u> having them now?

Timeline for experiences: Now, this month, this year

Experience	When to invest in it? (Now, this month, this year, next year)	Notes
Example: Run a marathon	Example: This year	Hire a trainer; join a gym.

Notes/insights from the above:

_____

_____

_____

_____

_____

Who do you want to join you?

Reflecting on the experiences you listed above, **who** do you want to join you? Consider the memory dividends that will come to you, based on having those experiences in the short term (rather than waiting), and sharing them with the people closest to you.

Of course, it's fine if some of those experiences are just for you. But also think about how some of them could be enriched by sharing them with the right people in your life.

Shared Experiences: Who do you want to join you?

Experience	Who do you want to join you?
Example: Run a marathon	Example: My brother and my son

Notes/insights from the above:

_____

_____

_____

_____

_____

Memory Dividends: How Can You Enhance Them?

Consider how you can proactively enhance your memory dividends.

For example:
- Would it help you create more vivid memories if you took more photos?
- Could you plan reunions with people you've shared good times with in the past?
- Could you create a video and send it to the group who participated in the experience?
- How about a photo album?

Other ideas to take your experiences to another level could be:
- Hiring a photographer
- Hiring a chef
- Staying somewhere beautiful / meaningful instead of 'normal'
- Picking a destination or experience based on criteria you know someone close to you will love
- Bringing older parents / relatives and making it easy for them to participate

Think about how you can actively enhance your memory dividends. Would it help you to take more photos of your experiences? To plan reunions with people you've shared good times with in the past? Compile a video or a photo album?

Shared Experiences: How can I really ramp up my memory dividends?

Experience	How can I enhance memory dividends?
Example: Run a marathon	Example: Recruit a friend to take lots of photos; meet my family afterwards for breakfast

Notes/insights from the above:

_____

_____

_____

_____

_____

Chapter 3. Why die with zero?

Rule No. 3: Aim to die with zero.

Worried About Dying With Zero?

If the idea of dying with zero still worries you, really reflect on where this psychological resistance comes from. For example:

- Are there lessons from your parents or grandparents that dying with zero isn't 'right', or is too risky?
- Is there unseen peer pressure from friends or colleagues that's making you nervous?
- Is it about what other people will think if you die with zero?
- Are you concerned about your legacy, and what you'll leave behind?
- Are you overly worried about future costs, and therefore not wanting to overspend in the present?
- There may be other things making you nervous. This is normal. Try to break it down and get to the bottom of them.

Below, explore the potential fears that might be holding you back from dying with zero. And keep in mind: when the book refers do dying with zero, it means:

- Not <u>exactly</u> zero, as this is impossible. But as close to it as you can reasonably get, such that you don't have wasted life energy (in the form of leftover money) that you haven't spent; and
- If you'd like to pass on an inheritance to kids or someone else, that by the time you die you'll ideally have <u>already done that</u>, so it becomes their money, not yours.

What's holding you back from planning your 'Die With Zero' strategy? And is there a counterpoint for each of these hesitations?

Examples:

- *"What about the kids?"* → As above, any inheritances would become *the recipient's* money, not yours. And this is covered in more detail in a later chapter.
- *I need to leave money when I die - for others.* → Would they not be better off to receive any inheritance *sooner*, when they might need it the most, rather than waiting until you die? Plus you'll get to see them use/spend/enjoy it while you're still alive, which is a benefit for you as well.
- *I'm scared I'll run out of money.* → This is a valid concern, and the balance is to have *enough*, without having *too much*.

Explore your own fears and hesitations, below:

Hesitation about Dying With Zero	Is there a counterpoint for this hesitation?
Example: Worried about what my kids will inherit	Example: Give them their inheritance NOW, when they're more likely to need it

Notes/insights from the above:

_____

_____

_____

_____

_____

_____

"But I love my job!" - Are you getting the most out of your non-work time?

Many people love their job - and that's fantastic. But, as the book points out, most people would still maximize the enjoyment of their life by having _at least some_ non-work time doing what they love.

Think about your own situation: If you love your job, in which ways could you spend time on other activities that *don't* involve working for money?

I could ramp up my enjoyment outside of work in the following ways:

1. _____

2. _____

3. _____

4. _____

5. _____

Notes/insights from the above:

_____

_____

_____

_____

_____

Are you rewarding yourself for your hard work?

In addition to the above - even if you love your job, *not* spending the money you earned while you were working (as even if you like it, you're still ultimately working for money) would still be a waste of life energy. Are you getting the maximum enjoyment out of the money you earn from your job, and in which other ways could you turn the dial up?

I think I could 'turn up' the enjoyment on the money I make from my job, in the following ways (e.g. take a trip, spend more time with family/friends, improve my health, etc.):

1. _____

2. _____

3. _____

4. _____

5. _____

Notes/insights from the above:

_____

_____

_____

_____

_____

How might you be over-compensating for later, and not quite living enough now?

As outlined in the book, many people over-save and over-compensate, due to:
- Good *intentions* to spend the money they've saved, but never actually doing it. This might be due to an inability to spend the money (lifelong thrifty habits that don't magically change when they get older), reduced desire to use it (less desire to travel in old age, for example), or other reasons.
- Overcaution, particularly with regard to unforeseen medical expenses towards the end of our lives.

In which ways might you be prone to, or concerned about, <u>over</u> saving for retirement?

1. _____

2. _____

3. _____

4. _____

5. _____

Notes/insights from the above:

_____

_____

_____

_____

_____

How can you fit your spending in with your work schedule?

If you really like your job and enjoy going to work every day, think about ways to spend your money and activities that fit comfortably within your work schedule.

Examples:
- Can you go to the gym before or after work?
- Can you plan more of your favorite activities on the weekend, instead of staying in?
- Can you take on slightly less at work, in order to have more energy before/after to spend on your favorite things?
- Can you meet with a friend during your lunch break, somewhere exciting, instead of just going to the cafeteria?
- Have you used all your annual leave days? If not, can you use some of those to act on more of your dream experiences <u>now</u>?

Ideas to fit spending within your work schedule:

Activity / Experience	Ways to fit this in with work schedule
Example: Marathon Training	Example: Run with a friend before work; take my gym bag and shower before I start.

Notes/insights from the above:

_____

_____

_____

_____

Chapter 4: How to spend your money (without actually hitting zero before you die)

Rule No. 4: Use all available tools to help you die with zero.

Life Expectancy Calculation

Try out one or more life expectancy calculators online. Two suggestions from the book are listed below, along with space to fill out your answers.

What do you notice? What stood out to you? Note your answers below.

→ **Right now I am _____ years old.**

1. **Exercise #1:** Based on the **Longevity Calculator at** longevityillustrator.org , I have a rough estimated probability of living to the following ages:

Note: The calculator will give you a table that looks exactly like this

Living to this age...	I have about this probability
65	___ %
70	___ %
75	___ %
80	___ %
85	___ %
90	___ %
95	___ %
100	___ %

2. **Exercise #2:** Based on the **Living to 100 Calculator at** livingto100.com, I have a rough idea of living to:

Age now	Living to 100 Calculator (rough idea)
65	____ %

Notes/insights from the above exercises:

_____

_____

_____

_____

Annuities: Helping With The Worry

If you're nervous about running out of money before you die, take some time to look into annuities as a possible solution.

Annuities research / notes:

_____

_____

_____

_____

Chapter 5: What about the kids?

Rule No. 5: Give money to your children or to charity when it has the most impact.

Giving: When Can I Have The Biggest Impact?

Think about which ages you'd like to give or leave money to your children, or other loved ones. How and when could that money have the most impact for them?

Also consider charities, if you'd like to give to them. Discuss in-depth with your spouse or partner if applicable to you.

Note: Also ensure you discuss these matters with an expert on the topic, such as a lawyer or estate planner. They can help you assess the financial impact, as well as firm up the legal details of what you'd like to give and when.

Who might I / we like to give money to, as part of an inheritance or charity?

Checklist

- ☐ Discuss with spouse or partner
- ☐ List recipients (people/charities), amounts and timing of when to give - <u>see below</u>
- ☐ Find an expert such as an estate planner or lawyer
- ☐ Assess the financial impact on me/us of giving money to others
- ☐ Assess the legal requirements of giving money to others
- ☐ Make the transactions

Who? Person / charity we'd like to give to	How much? Amount we'd like to give	When? When would have the biggest impact for them?

Notes/insights from the above:

_____

_____

_____

_____

_____

_____

_____

Your Legacy Is More Than Just Money

Your legacy might involve some kind of monetary inheritance, but Bill Perkins also encourages us to think about <u>other</u> ways in which we can leave a legacy behind. Things like:

- Memories
- Experiences
- Time together

In which ways -- <u>outside of money</u> -- would you like to leave a legacy to those you care about? Putting some proactive, concrete thought behind this can help you craft an intentional legacy as you go.

Who? People important to my legacy	**What form?** Time together, shared experiences, etc	**How?** How can I do / plan for this in a concrete, deliberate way?

Notes/insights from the above:

_____

_____

_____

_____

Chapter 6: Balance your life

Rule No. 6: Don't live your life on autopilot.

What Could I Do Now, But (Maybe) Not Later?

Consider your physical health currently. What life experiences could you have now that you might not be able to have if you postpone them?

Experiences I'd like to prioritize to do now / soon:

Experience	Why is it best done now?	What would happen if I postponed it? (Cost of inaction)
Example: Scuba diving in Galapagos Islands	Example: Respiratory health declines with age; work will get busier	Example: May not be able to do it due to health decline and/or other commitments

Notes/insights from the above:

_____

_____

_____

_____

Health As #1: How Can You Improve Everything Else?

Health is often the number one thing we can do to 'move the needle' on enjoyment of *everything* else in life. What's one way you could invest time and/or money into improving your health, and thereby improve *all* of your life experiences in the future?

Try to be really specific about it, so you can turn it into an action. Some examples could be:
- I can exercise 3 times per week for 45 minutes
- I can hire a personal trainer to help me stay on track
- I can improve my diet to eating well 80% of the time
- I can start a yoga class twice per week
- I can begin the practice of meditation
- I can prioritize sleep over watching TV

These (above) are just some examples. Not down some of your own ideas of how you could improve your health. Then pick just <u>one</u> key thing to start, today.

Ideas: How I Could Improve My Health

| |
| |
| |
| |
| |
| |
| |

What's the <u>ONE</u> idea you picked to start with <u>TODAY</u>?

_____

Reading: A Key To Health Improvements

Improving your eating habits can be life-changing - and one of the best ways is to read some books on the subject. Of the many books out there, my favorite is Eat To Live by Joel Furhman, M.D.

Spend a few minutes asking friends or researching some books on healthy, sustainable, long-term eating. What grabs your interest? Purchase 1 or 2 of them and get reading, as this is one of the biggest things you can do to improve your health.

Books I'd like to read about health eating / diet:

Book Title & Author	Why did it grab my attention?	Purchased?
Example: Eat To Live by Joel Furhman	Example: Recommended in Die With Zero; reviews look good	✓

Notes/insights from the above:

_____

_____

_____

_____

Physical Activity Map

Increasing physical activities is another way to improve long-term health and enjoyment of future experiences. Here we're talking about doing *more* of what physical activities that you *already* enjoy (examples: dancing, hiking, walking, running).

What do I already do, that I'd like to do <u>more of</u>?:

Activity	How could I do more of this?
Example: Hiking in the mountains	Example: Book a hike every 2 weeks; invite a friend to join me; get new boots

Notes/insights from the above:

_____

_____

_____

Need some more time? Brainstorm - Freeing Up Time

If your ability to enjoy unique experiences is constrained more by time than by money (or health), brainstorm some ways to free up time.

Could you hire a cleaner to clean your house, freeing up valuable hours? Could you hire a cook, or have food delivered, to free up time for experiences? And so-on.

Brainstorm some ideas, then pick one or two to implement this week.

How could I free up time?

Activity	How could I do more of this?
Example: House cleaning - 2 hours per week	Example: Hire a cleaner to clean the house so I can go hiking instead

What are the 1-2 ideas you picked to start with TODAY?

_____

_____

Chapter 7: Start to time bucket your life

Rule No. 7: Think of your life as distinct seasons.

Carefully Crafted Time Buckets

Time-bucket your life, as described in the book. The main goal here is not to over-complicate or try to plan everything; but rather, to give a <u>simple</u> view of considering different life stages. What you want to do at the age of 25-30 will be different to what you want to do when you are 75-80, both in terms of desire, and also in terms of physical ability.

If time-bucketing your whole life feels a bit overwhelming, just do the exercise with three time buckets covering the next 30 years. Know you can always add more to your list; just do it long before your age and health become a real factor.

What are the main activities you'd like to do, in the following buckets?

Remember that more physically demanding activities might be better suited to earlier phases (you'll be skiing less or not at all when you're 80), whereas some activities can be done at mostly any phase (museum visits, library research, etc.).

Age Bracket	Experiences
25-30 years old	Examples: Volunteer in Africa, hike the Inca Trail
40-45 years old	
46-50 years old	

Continued on next page →

51-60 years old	
60-74 years old	
75-80 years old	

Notes/insights from the above:

_____

_____

_____

_____

Before They Get Too Old: Shared Experiences with The kids

If you have children, consider your own version of the Heffalump movie (mentioned in the book): What are 1-2 experiences you want more of with your kids in the next two years, before that phase comes to an end?

Brainstorm of experiences I'd like to increase with my kids

Activity	Note
Example: Disneyland visit	Example: They've always wanted to go and will soon be too old to care about it

What are the <u>1-2</u> ideas you picked to start with <u>TODAY</u>?

_____

_____

Chapter 8: Know your peak

Rule No. 8: Know when to stop growing your wealth.

Calculate your annual survival cost based on where you plan to live in retirement.

First: Some fact-finding

To do this, we need to know:

1. Our cost of living per year, or <u>projected</u> cost of living for later in life. To calculate the cost of living 1 year, you may need to do some research, depending on:
    *   Where you want to live
    *   The lifestyle that interests you - e.g. more or less travel; higher VS lower rent/mortgage, etc.
    *   You can use current expenses as a guideline/starting point if unsure.

2. How many years we have left to live. To find this out:
    *   You can use the life expectancy calculators from earlier chapters as a guideline.
    *   In addition, consult your doctor to get a read on your biological age and mortality; get all the objective tests you can afford that give you the status of your current health and eventual decline.

Then we follow a two-step calculation, as outlined in the book:

Step 1: *Cost of living 1 year x years left to live.* For example, if it costs you $12,000 per year to live, and you're currently 45 and plan to live until 85, you would end up with:

12,000 x 40 years = $480,000.

But, recall that this number doesn't take into account:
A) You earning interest on the principal you are saving;
B) Inflation; and
C) That the cost of living generally *decreases* as we get older - past a certain point when we settle down and have less desire to do more physical activities.

Which leads us to....

Step 2: Based on the guideline in the book, you would need approximately 70% of the initial estimate in step 1 above. Why? Because the interest you earn (example: 5%) will help to offset inflation (example: 3%) and will mean you actually need less.

This leads us to the calculation for step 2, the 'survival threshold' from the book:

0.7 x (cost of living 1 year) x years left to live

My numbers:

Cost of living 1 year	Years left to live

Next: Let's Calculate
Now that you've got your two numbers, above, let's do the two calculations:

Step 1 calculation:
Cost of living 1 year x years left to live

Mine: _____ x _____ = $ _____ required

Step 2 calculation: Taking into account inflation and potential interest,
0.7 x (cost of living 1 year) x years left to live

Mine: 0.7 x _____ x _____ = $ _____ required

Notes/insights from the above:

_____

_____

_____

_____

How might my health impact my favorite activities over my lifetime?

Given your own health and history, think about when your enjoyment of those activities is likely to start declining in a noticeable way on an annual basis - and how the activities you love will be affected by this decline.

My favorite activities which might be impacted by health:

Activity	Impacted by health? If so, how?
Example: Running marathons	Example: I'm 40 now; my knees hurt. I may need to shorten distances or find other hobbies at 45-50
Example: Long-haul traveling	Example: I'm 40 now; I'm still good to do long-haul travel for another 10-20 years at least

Notes/insights from the above:

_____

_____

_____

Calculate your peak (hint: it's a date, not a number)

Recall from the book that Bill Perkins says that your peak is a <u>date</u>, not a number. This is the financial 'peak' or high-point of your life, and can be a good time to break open the nest-egg you've saved up. Here we should take into account not only a monetary number (dollar value), but <u>also</u> free time and health, the other two pillars of enjoyment.

This leads us to identifying the ability to enjoy experiences, based on:
- Level of wealth (do you have enough money to enjoy it?); and
- Physical ability (are you physically able-bodied enough to enjoy it?)

For most people, this date seems to be between 45 to 60 years old, and it is tied to your <u>biological</u> age. If you're healthy, the peak might be on the later end of this scale, as you're likely to live longer and therefore will peak later in your life.

Lastly, recall that this is not (necessarily) your retirement number; but rather, the time when you should start <u>spending more than you earn</u>, in order to die with zero and not have leftover money (and therefore life energy) sitting in the bank that you never used during your lifetime.

Consider the following thought experiments:
- On a scale of 1-10, how 'healthy' do you consider yourself to be?

    _____

- Have you had your <u>biological</u> age measured with a doctor? If yes, what is it?

    _____

- At which age do you plan to retire?

    _____

- What are some <u>key experiences</u> you'd like to have later in life, after you break open your nest egg?

  _____

  _____

  _____

- Based on the information above, as well as this chapter in the book, roughly where do you think your peak would be, relatively to the recommended 'peak' range of 45-60? (Tick one)

  [ ] Earlier side (e.g. 45-50)
  [ ] Mid range (e.g. 50-55)
  [ ] Later side (e.g. 55-60)

As the exact peak age is intensely personal, based on a range of factors like biological age, annual income, investments, interest rates, health, planned retirement spending and more, it's not possible to calculate an *exact* peak date for everyone, via the book or these exercises. But using the information above should give you an approximation of when you might want to start optimizing for experience and *spending more than you earn*, so you don't end up with too much unused money left in the bank.

Optional: Consult a financial advisor to help you drill down into more specific numbers and help you determine a 'peak' date. Some information to take to them could include:
- Your actual age
- Your biological age (from your doctor)
- Current income, savings and investments (your net worth)
- Any inheritances you plan to give
- Planned retirement annual spending - try to time bucket this if possible, for example:
  - 50-60: Annual spending of $X based on planned experiences & health
  - 60-70: Annual spending of $Y based on planned experiences & health
  - 70-80: Annual spending of $Z based on planned experiences & health

Notes/insights from the above:

_____

Chapter 9: Be bold not foolish

Rule No. 9: Take your biggest risks when you have little to lose.

Identify opportunities that you're not taking that pose little to risk to you. Always remember that you're better off taking more chances when you are younger than when you're older.

What am I holding on right now that is low risk with potential high reward?

Activity	Impacted by health? If so, how?
Example: Running marathons	Example: I'm 40 now; my knees hurt, I may need to shorten distances or find other hobbies at 45-50
Example: Long-haul traveling	Example: I'm 40 now; I'm still good to do long-haul travel for another 10-20 years at least

Notes/insights from the above:

_____

_____

_____

What Fears Are Holding Me Back?
Examine the fears that could be holding you back. These might be rational fears, or they might be deep-seated, ingrained or irrational fears. By becoming aware of them, you can often start to move past them and process them. The goal: Not to let irrational fears get in the way of dreaming big and accomplishing all you want to accomplish.

Your Risk Profile
Thinking about your own risk tolerance, based on your age and comfort levels, where would you place yourself on the following rough scale?

[ ] Low Risk Tolerance. I prefer to know exactly what's happening and when, and plan most things down to a great level of detail. I'm ok with taking lower risks in return for potentially lower rewards, because that feels more comfortable for me.

[ ] Medium Risk Tolerance. I'm ok with taking calculated risks after some thought and consideration. I feel most comfortable with medium-to-low risk levels, in return for medium-to-low returns.

[ ] High Risk Tolerance. Go big or go home. I'm young and have time to recover from risky situations, and/or I have a high preference for taking bigger risks for the potential of a higher reward.

What fears come up for you? *As this is a more involved exercise, we've provided some longer examples.*

Examples:

Fear	Rational or Irrational? Where does it come from? Lastly, what could you do to offset this fear?
Example: Running out of money if I quit my job I don't like.	Example: We didn't have a lot of money growing up. Now that I have some, I'm afraid that if I Lose it, I won't get it back. But I have a high-paying job, lots of savings, and low expenses. I'm only 25; I could easily recover if I needed to.
Example: If I move to my dream destination, I might not like it.	Example: I have a good routine at home. Even though I dream of moving to X place, I'm scared of what might happen if it doesn't work out. On the other hand, I could always come back home and be set up again within 1-3 months if it didn't go well.

Now examine your own fears:

Fear	Rational or Irrational? Where does it come from? Lastly, what could you do to offset this fear?

Notes/insights from the above:

Recognise that you have choices at every moment. Ideally we want these choices to reflect your priorities - try to examine your choices and make them deliberately, rather than on-the-fly or 'going with the flow'. To help with this, think about the 5 most recent medium to large decisions you've made in the last 6 months. Did they reflect your values and what's important to you?

Examples:

Choice I made	Did it reflect my values? Why?
Example: Choosing to spend an extra $1,000 on a trip, to extend it by 5 days to spend with my family.	Example: Yes. Family and travel are huge values for me. Spending this extra money allowed me to do both, which felt good and aligned with what's important to me.
Example: Choosing to buy a car that was $5,000 over my initial budget.	Example: Not really. Fancy cars aren't very important to me. I think I let myself be talked into it by the salesperson. This didn't align 100% with my values. (This is ok because I can always change my car later; I can learn and move on).

Now examine your own recent 5 medium-to-large choices in the last 6 months:

Choice I made	Did it reflect my values? Why?

Notes/insights from the above:

_____

_____

_____

_____

You made it to the end!

Thank you.

Thank you so much for picking up the Workbook for Bill Perkins' *Die With Zero*. We really hope you enjoyed it, and that it helped you internalize, plan and put the lessons into practice.

If you'd like to give feedback on the book, or to find more workbooks for other self-development books, join us at BigActionBooks.com.

Thanks again,
The Big Action Books team

BigActionBooks.com

Notes:

_____

_____

_____

_____

_____

_____

_____

_____

_____

_____

_____

_____

_____

_____

Notes:

Notes:

_____

_____

_____

_____

_____

_____

_____

_____

_____

_____

_____

_____

_____

_____

_____

_____

Notes:

Notes:

_____

_____

_____

_____

_____

_____

_____

_____

_____

_____

_____

_____

_____

_____

Made in United States
Troutdale, OR
01/28/2024

17251609R00029